3-3/2014-2/15
6 - 4/2016- 7/16
9 -8/2017-3/18

D0531985

THE U.S. ARMED FORCES

TODAY'S U.S. NAVY

by DON NARDO

Consultant:
Raymond L. Puffer, PhD
Historian, Retired
Edwards Air Force Base History Office

COMPASS POINT BOOKS
a capstone imprint

Compass Point Books are published by Capstone,
1710 Roe Crest Drive, North Mankato, Minnesota 56003
www.capstonepub.com

Editorial Credits
Editor: Brenda Haugen
Designer: Alison Thiele
Production Specialist: Eric Manske
Library Consultant: Kathleen Baxter

Photo Credits
Corbis, 6, Bettmann, 23, 39, Oscar White, 40, Sygma/Jacques Langevin, 41; DoD photo, 43; NARA,
5; Newscom: Rob Crandall Stock Connection Worldwide, 21, ZUMA Press, 17; U.S. Naval History
and Heritage Command, 38; U.S. Navy Photo, 10, MC2 James R. Evans, 8, MC2 Jeffrey Richardson,
15, MC2 Julia A. Casper, 30, MC2 Mark Logico, 33, MC2 Meranda Keller, 18, MC2 Micah P.
Blechner, 28, MC2 Michelle Kapica, 34, MC3 Benjamin Crossley, 29, MC3 Scott Pittman, 13, MCC
Stan Travioli, 36, MCSA Brian H. Abel, 7, MCSN Adam Randolph, cover (top), MCSN Corey R.
Oesch, cover (bottom), 1, PHC Eric A. Clement, 14, Scott A. Thornbloom, 26, Sue Krawczyk, 22, 25,
Missile Defense Agency, 32; U.S. Navy SEAL and SWCC photo, 35

Artistic Effects
Shutterstock: doodle, Ewa Walicka, Kilmukhametov Art, Nova Development Corporation, W.J.

Library of Congress Cataloging-in-Publication Data
Nardo, Don, 1947–
  Today's U.S. Navy/by Don Nardo, consultant, Raymond L. Puffer.
     p. cm. – (U.S. Armed Forces)
  Audience: Grades 4-6.
  Includes bibliographical references and index.
  ISBN 978-0-7565-4617-5 (library binding)
  ISBN 978-0-7565-4641-0 (paperback)
  ISBN 978-0-7565-4676-2 (eBook pdf)
  1. United States. Navy—Juvenile literature. I. Puffer, Raymond L. II. Title.
  VA58.4.N37 2013
  359.00973—dc23   2012023144

Printed in the United States of America in Brainerd, Minnesota.
092012   006938BANGS13

TABLE OF
CONTENTS

CHAPTER ONE:
A FEARSOME FORCE

Today's U.S. Navy is part of a long and proud tradition. Its history is filled with acts of heroism. And though their actions don't always make the evening news, the brave men and women of the U.S. Navy continue to be tested around the world. From fighting terrorism to combating piracy, U.S. Navy seamen put their lives on the line to keep others safe.

Among the most important days in naval history was Sunday, December 7, 1941. At Pearl Harbor, on the Hawaiian island of Oahu, the start of the day was quiet. Most of the warships of the U.S. Pacific fleet were docked there. There were 96 vessels in all. Some of the American sailors were eating breakfast. Others were alseep or preparing to attend church.

Around 8 a.m. a sailor aboard the USS *Maryland* saw something in the distance.

He later recalled:

"I noticed planes diving on the Naval Air Base nearby. At first I thought they were our planes just in mock diving practice attack. But [then] I saw smoke and flames rising from a building. I looked closer and saw that they were not American planes."

Those planes turned out to be Japanese. More than 350 of them attacked the American fleet that morning. For almost two hours, death and destruction rained from the sky. When it was over, naval personnel inspected the grim scene. Twenty-one U.S. ships had been sunk or badly damaged. More than 300 American planes had been damaged or destroyed. Even worse, 2,403 Americans lay dead. Another 1,178 had been wounded.

The USS *Shaw* exploded during the Japanese attack on Pearl Harbor.

Most Japanese leaders thought they had permanently crippled the U.S. Navy. But they were wrong. American naval yards and factories rose to the challenge. They rapidly built new ships. By the thousands those vessels poured into the Pacific Ocean. In fewer than four years the Navy, aided by other U.S. forces, brought Japan to its knees. The Japanese formally surrendered September 2, 1945. That ended the Pacific portion of World War II.

Ever since Japan's defeat, the U.S. Navy has been the world's leading naval force. In fact, after World War II the U.S. Navy was so huge and powerful that no other nation dared to attack it. In many ways World War II made the Navy what it is today.

THE BIRTH OF THE NAVY

The roots of the U.S. Navy lie in the American Revolution. In 1775 fighting began between Britain and its American colonies. The colonists responded in part by creating the Continental Navy. At its height it had 65 ships. Their main task was to disrupt British sea trade and operations. The Navy's first commander-in-chief was Esek Hopkins (above).

SIZE OF THE NAVY

The Navy is one of several branches of America's military. The main purpose of all the branches is to defend the United States.

The Navy is the largest American sea-based force. So when enemy ships, or planes from those ships, threaten, the Navy swings into action. It takes the lead in the sea segments of all the nation's wars.

Members of the Navy take that duty and their jobs seriously. When asked, they are proud to state their overall mission—"to maintain, train, and equip combat-ready naval forces capable of winning wars." The Navy also deters aggression and maintains the freedom of the seas.

The size of the U.S. Navy has varied over the years. It was at its biggest during World War II. About 4.2 million Americans served in the Navy during that conflict. By the end of the war, the Navy had more than

**U.S. sailors on a mission
in Yokosuka, Japan**

6,700 ships. More than 30 of them were aircraft carriers.

Today the Navy is smaller, but it's the largest and strongest naval force in the world. It has 285 ships in active service. It also has more than 3,700 warplanes. In 2012 the Navy had about 324,000 active sailors, including 54,000 women.

The Navy also had about 106,000 backup sailors who belong to the U.S. Navy Reserve. Usually these sailors serve one weekend a month. They also train for two weeks once each year. In an emergency some or all of them might have to serve full time.

Boxes of food are passed up a ladder on an aircraft carrier.

NAVY CULTURE

Americans who join the Navy quickly get used to its culture, its way of life. Sailors spend much of their time at sea, so they use many special terms relating to ships and the ocean.

Midships means the middle section of a ship, for example. BS means battle stations. A stairway on a ship is called a ladder. A waft is a signal flag, and a sailor's bed is his or her rack. Another habit sailors must get into is saluting officers, who are referred to as sir or ma'am.

Still another aspect of Navy culture, and all branches of the military, is using military time to denote the hours in a day. The military uses a 24-hour clock that begins at midnight. So 3 p.m., for example, is 1500 hours. In addition, they use the military alphabet in some communications. That alphabet has the same letters as the regular English alphabet. But each letter has a word to express it. For instance, the word for A is Alpha. The word for T is Tango, and the one for V is Victor. So the word "vat" would be expressed as "Victor Alpha Tango." This is done to make the words in messages as clear as possible.

MILITARY TIME • • • • • • • • • • • • • • • • •

All branches of the military use military time. Civilian time runs from 12 midnight to 12 noon. Then it goes through another 12-hour cycle. In contrast, military time is based on a 24-hour day. Some times of the day in both systems are listed below.

Civilian	Military
12 a.m., or midnight	0000, or zero, zero, zero, zero
3 a.m.	0300, or oh-three-hundred hours
6 a.m.	0600, or oh-six-hundred hours
9 a.m.	0900, or oh-nine-hundred hours
12 p.m., or noon	1200, or twelve-hundred hours
3 p.m.	1500, or fifteen-hundred hours
6 p.m.	1800, or eighteen-hundred hours
9 p.m.	2100, or twenty-one-hundred hours

CHAPTER TWO:
NAVY ORGANIZATION AND JOBS

The U.S. Navy is extremely well organized and efficient. Because it is so efficient, its chances of success are high. Since the Navy was founded in 1775, almost all of its missions have succeeded.

One key aspect of Navy organization is its well-ordered chain of command. Its chief aim is to allow Navy leaders to pass orders quickly and effectively to those who will carry out those orders. The U.S. military's top leaders are civilians. This is because the country is a democracy. Having civilians in charge helps to keep the military from having too much power over U.S. citizens. The leader of the Navy is the president. Beneath the president are two more civilians. One is the secretary of defense. The other is the secretary of the Navy.

Next in the chain of command is the highest ranking Navy officer—the chief of naval operations. Then come the admirals. Each admiral oversees a fleet or squadron of ships. Beneath the admirals are the

Ray Mabus, the 75th secretary of the Navy

captains, who command those ships. The ranks of lieutenant and ensign follow.

Directly below the officers in the command chain are the enlisted sailors. The highest ranked among them are the petty officers. Finally come the seamen. The uniform of each Navy sailor bears an insignia to show his or her rank. Only the seamen recruits, the lowest ranking seaman, wear no rank insignia.

THE NAVY CHAIN OF COMMAND • • • • • • • • • • •

Civilians
President of the United States
Secretary of Defense
Secretary of the Navy
Officers
Chief of Naval Operations (an admiral)
Admiral (followed by vice admiral and rear admiral)
Captain
Commander (followed by lieutenant commander)
Lieutenant (followed by lieutenant, junior grade)
Ensign
Enlisted
Master chief petty officer (followed by senior chief and chief petty officers)
Petty officer first class (followed by second and third class petty officers)
Seaman (followed by seaman apprentice and seaman recruit)

STRUCTURE OF THE NAVY

The U.S. Navy's operating forces are also well organized. They consist mainly of several large units called Operations Forces. One is called the Fleet Forces Command, which is sometimes referred to as the Atlantic Fleet. Two of the others are Naval Forces Europe and the Naval Special Warfare Command.

Within some of these large units are smaller ones called fleets. Each is assigned to a specific region in the world. A fleet consists of all of the Navy ships in that region.

Each fleet is made up of several task forces, which are large groups of vessels of assorted types. Each task force usually has one or more naval squadrons. A squadron consists of a few large-scale ships, called capital ships, such as aircraft carriers. Also within a task force are one or more flotillas. A flotilla is made up of a few smaller vessels, called noncapital vessels. Finally, the smallest naval unit is a single ship.

In wartime these units can be used in many combinations. A certain combination might be best for one situation. While another situation might call for a different grouping of vessels. This gives the Navy a lot of flexibility. It helps make the Navy very efficient and powerful.

The sailors who serve in the various naval units perform numerous jobs. In the words of one of those sailors, the Navy "offers careers and jobs that fit all backgrounds and interests. There are literally hundreds of distinct professional roles in dozens of exciting fields."

Ships with the Enterprise Carrier Strike Group traveled in formation while crossing the Atlantic Ocean.

The Navy offers so many different jobs because it takes many people and their talents to run each ship. An aircraft carrier requires a crew of nearly 6,000, counting the pilots and crews of the airplanes onboard. Even the smallest warship, a frigate, has a crew of more than 200.

The men and women must have a wide range of skills. Navigators plot a vessel's course. They are aided by computer operators. There are also several kinds of engineers and mechanics onboard a vessel. They maintain and repair weapons and boilers. They also work on fighter

Sailors on the bridge of the USS *Theodore Roosevelt*

A weather balloon is launched from an aircraft carrier in the Arabian Gulf.

DAMAGE CONTROL

planes, helicopters, and much more. In addition, the ships that have planes and helicopters need pilots to fly them. Just a few of the many other Navy jobs are communications expert, weather expert, mapmaker, doctor, nurse, and chef. The Navy has a high percentage of the same jobs that exist outside the military.

One of the most important tasks on a Navy ship is preventing and fighting fires. That job is called damage control. Those who do the job maintain and operate firefighting equipment. They are also in charge of chemical, biological, and radioactive materials. It is vital to keep those substances contained in a safe manner.

CHAPTER THREE:
ENLISTING
IN THE NAVY

In 1936 millions of people flocked to see the movie musical *Follow the Fleet*. It featured a rousing song that began with the words: "We joined the Navy to see the world. And what did we see? We saw the sea!" The composer took some of those words from a famous Navy recruiting poster. It read, "Join the Navy and see the world."

The song's lyrics were meant as a joke. Some sailors in the movie joined the Navy so they could travel far and wide. But they ended up seeing nothing but water. In real life, however, many sailors do travel to faraway, interesting cities and countries. Today that remains one of the main reasons people enlist in the Navy.

Some people decide at an early age that they want to join the Navy. So when they are old enough, they visit Navy recruiters.

The recruiters interview them and help them sign up for Navy service. But in many other cases, recruiters go looking for people. Military officer Scott A. Ostrow explains why. The military must attract thousands of new recruits each year, he says. This is so the Navy can maintain a high level of readiness. Finding enough new recruits also ensures the military can perform its mission, he says.

In whatever way a person decides to enlist, he or she must go through a set process. The Navy first checks to confirm the applicant is old enough. Applicants must be at least 18 years old, but a 17-year-old can enlist with a parent's permission.

A Navy recruiter talks with a possible enlistee in Texas.

The U.S. Navy sponsored the 18th annual Hispanic Track and Field games in New York in 2012.

Being in good physical condition is important too. After measuring an applicant's height and weight, an examiner checks the applicant's vision and hearing. Blood and urine tests are also done. When deemed necessary, X-rays or other tests are given as well.

If the applicant passes the physical exam, he or she must also pass a background check. This is to make sure that the person does not have a serious criminal record. Navy investigators look into the applicant's past. They contact the schools he or she attended. They also talk to the police in the person's town. Finally, the applicant is fingerprinted.

The Navy also tests all applicants to find out about their talents and abilities. The exam is called the ASVAB, which stands for Armed Services Vocational Aptitude Battery. It consists of multiple-choice questions and lasts up to four hours. The test shows how strong a person's reading and math skills are. It also shows if he or she has mechanical or other abilities.

A few applicants score extremely low on the ASVAB. For the moment they are not allowed to enlist, but they can retake the test later. This doesn't happen very often, however. The test helps both the Navy and the applicant. The Navy is able to place the person in a job for which

he or she is well suited. That increases the organization's efficiency. Also, the applicant gets to perform a job that uses his or her talents. It is less likely, therefore, that the person will be bored or unhappy.

NO DRUGS ALLOWED

Applicants for the Navy are tested for illegal drugs on a random basis. Anyone who fails the test cannot join, although he or she can retake the test later. Illegal drug use is not allowed. In addition, all sailors are retested for drugs from time to time. One reason for this is to make sure sailors are as healthy as possible. Also, someone who is on drugs can endanger other sailors and make a mission fail.

"I DO SWEAR"

When the enlistee has met all the requirements, it is time to make joining the Navy official. This step involves taking an oath.

Everyone who does so views it as a serious, highly important moment. The person realizes that his or her life is about to change in many ways.

A Navy officer conducts the ceremony. The officer stands beside an American flag and faces the enlistee. The latter then raises his or her right hand and says:

"I do solemnly swear that I will support and defend the Constitution of the United States against all enemies, foreign and domestic; that I will bear true faith and allegiance to the same; and that I will obey the orders of the President of the United States and the orders of the officers appointed over me, according to regulations and the Uniform Code of Military Justice. So help me God."

New recruits in Boston, Massachusetts, are sworn in.

CHAPTER **FOUR:**

TRAINING TO BECOME A SAILOR

Once a person has joined the Navy, the first stop is basic training. Lasting seven weeks, it is also called boot camp. Sailors in training are referred to as recruits. Their memorable boot camp experiences take place at the Recruit Training Command (RTC). It is located at the Naval Station Great Lakes, near Waukegan, Illinois. More than 50,000 recruits pass through the facility near Chicago each year.

Male and female recruits train together at the RTC, but they are housed separately. During their stay they live in dormlike buildings nicknamed ships. Each ship has hundreds of beds and lockers. It also features communal bathrooms. Recruits are expected to keep their living quarters spotless and "shipshape."

An officer talks with recruits in their barracks, which are nicknamed ships.

WOMEN IN THE NAVY ● ● ● ● ● ● ● ● ● ● ● ● ● ● ● ●

Beginning in the American Revolution in the 1770s, women have served in all U.S. wars. At first they could not formally join the Navy or Army. But several women served as nurses. They cared for wounded sailors and soldiers. A few women even fought in battle by pretending to be men. During World War I around 13,000 women worked in Navy Department offices. In 1942, during World War II, Congress created the WAVES. It stood for Women Accepted for Volunteer Emergency Service. Navy WAVES served in dozens of noncombat jobs during the war, including mechanic, radio operator, electrician, and air-traffic controller. In the decades that followed, female roles in the Navy expanded. In 1976 the Naval Academy at Annapolis began accepting female cadets. On May 28, 1980, Elizabeth Belzer became the first woman to graduate from the United States Naval Academy (above). Over time woman gained the right to serve on all Navy ships except submarines. That barrier fell in 2010, when women were allowed to serve as officers on subs.

At the start of boot camp, the recruits divide into groups called divisions. Each division has 80 or more members. They train together for the entire seven weeks. Some of the initial training occurs in a classroom. There the recruits learn about the chain of command and how to show respect to officers. They are also taught the Navy's traditional customs and rules of conduct.

In addition, the recruits learn to identify every kind of ship in the Navy's fleets. Finally they memorize the Sailors Creed:

"I am a United States Sailor. I will support and defend the Constitution of the United States of America and I will obey the orders of those appointed over me. I represent the fighting spirit of the Navy and those who have gone before me to defend freedom and democracy around the world. I proudly serve my country's Navy combat team with Honor, Courage and Commitment. I am committed to excellence and the fair treatment of all."

Next the recruits go into the field for physical training. They do large numbers of sit-ups and pushups. They also climb ropes and run long distances. These and other exercises are designed to get them into the best shape possible.

The recruits often drill and march together. This helps them gain a better

sense of teamwork. Especially important is learning how to fight fires aboard a ship. A major fire could kill many sailors and render a vessel helpless.

Recruits go through rigorous physical fitness training.

Officer candidates face tough scrutiny from their instructors during Officer Candidate School in Rhode Island.

Near the end of boot camp, the recruits take part in "Battle Stations." It is a sort of final exam in which they show off what they have learned. One military officer says, "All of the training you receive [in] Recruit Training culminates in this event." The recruits complete difficult tasks that test their endurance and ability to work as a team.

When they graduate from boot camp, the recruits become sailors with the rank of seaman. If they work hard, they may earn promotions over time. They even have a

they graduate they have the rank of ensign.

Those who want to become officers have another option. It is to attend the United States Naval Academy at Annapolis, Maryland. Getting in is not easy. One has to be recommended by a member of the U.S. Congress or other responsible person. Even then only one in every 10 applicants is accepted. Training lasts four years. As might be expected, some of the training takes place aboard one or more ships or smaller boats.

ADVANCED TRAINING

chance of becoming officers someday.

But there are faster ways to reach that goal. One route to a career as a Navy officer is to go to Officer Candidate School (OCS). It is located in Newport, Rhode Island. In a 12-week program, the officer candidates study math, navigation, and how ships work. They also learn how to lead others. When

After boot camp enlisted sailors receive more advanced training. It takes place on the job. Each sailor masters the basics of an occupation. The Navy has hundreds of jobs from which to pick. Some sailors apprentice with more experienced naval personnel. Others work in on-duty training centers called "A" schools.

CHAPTER FIVE:
NAVY GEAR, SHIPS, AND WEAPONS

The warships and weapons used by the U.S. Navy are both powerful and effective. The ships come in all sizes, and they carry a wide array of destructive devices. Among these are missiles, torpedoes, warplanes, and attack helicopters. The Navy also supplies its sailors with effective gear. It consists of the special clothing and equipment they use when on duty.

Sailors' uniforms differ from those of Army soldiers. This is because soldiers often fight an enemy hand-to-hand, and they must wear armor and other protective clothing. But most sailors work aboard ships. They don't often meet the enemy up close. Therefore they usually wear pants, shirts, and jackets.

A pilot is given the "go-ahead" signal on an aircraft carrier in the Atlantic Ocean.

In some cases Navy clothes are color-coded. On an aircraft carrier, for instance, sailors who move the warplanes around wear yellow jerseys. Sailors who refuel the planes wear purple jerseys. Sailors who work with the bombs the planes carry wear red jerseys.

Sometimes the sailors who work with the planes must wear protective gear. When planes are taking off or landing, strong gusts of wind stir up. These can

A fuel hose is carried to aircraft aboard the USS _John C. Stennis._

knock sailors down or even overboard. So the men and women on deck don special safety gear. It includes heavy-duty helmets, goggles to protect the eyes, and life jackets. The deck crewmen also wear ear protection because of the loudness of the jet engines.

Another difference between Army and Navy gear involves firearms. In wartime soldiers carry rifles and often pistols. But most sailors do not carry firearms aboard a ship. Officers sometimes keep pistols in their personal safes in their cabins. Usually the only other person who has a gun on a vessel is the master-at-arms. He or she is the ship's police officer. The average small Navy vessel has one master-at-arms. But

The aircraft carrier USS *Dwight D. Eisenhower* during training in the Atlantic Ocean

for nearly 6,000 sailors and 60 or more warplanes. A carrier usually travels with an escort of smaller warships to protect it. Together these vessels make up a task force, which is also called a battle group.

The aircraft carriers have several possible missions. One is used in peacetime. It is to travel near the shores of a nation that poses a threat to the United States. This is called showing the flag. It tells that nation that the U.S. can and will use force if need be. During wartime carriers can perform a different mission—sending their planes to bomb enemy targets.

The planes and their bombs are the carriers' chief weapons. One of these aircraft is the F/A-18 Hornet. It attacks enemy planes and ground targets. Another type of plane, the E-2C Hawkeye, seeks out enemy ships and planes. The aircraft have very large ranges, from 500 to 800 miles (805 to 1,287 kilometers).

larger ships have more. Each aircraft carrier has more than 60.

Aircraft carriers are the largest ships in the U.S. Navy. Each is more than 1,000 feet (305 meters) long. It has room

The smaller ships in a task force are cruisers, destroyers, and frigates. The biggest of the three, a cruiser, has a great deal of firepower. It can do more than just guard a carrier. A cruiser can attack enemy aircraft, ships, and ground positions on its own.

The chief weapon in a cruiser's arsenal is the Tomahawk cruise missile. Each is about 20 ½ feet (6.2 m) long and travels at 550 miles (885 km) per hour. Cruise missiles are very accurate. One of them can hit a house hundreds of miles from the ship that fires it.

Destroyers and frigates are smaller than cruisers and are very fast. This allows them to chase and destroy enemy ships and submarines. Some destroyers carry cruise missiles. All have other missiles that can blow up enemy ships and missiles. Destroyers also feature large cannonlike deck guns. Frigates carry attack helicopters and torpedoes.

The Navy has submarines as well. Some are about 360 feet (110 m) long and carry a crew of 140. Many of the subs have both torpedoes and cruise missiles. Some have Trident missiles. Tridents can carry large-scale explosives and even nuclear warheads.

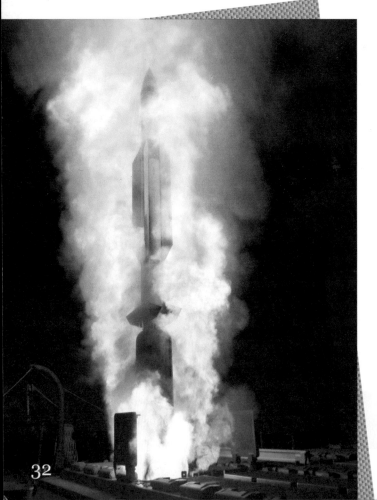

A missile is launched from the USS *Lake Erie* during testing.

A guided-missile cruiser followed a submarine during training near Hawaii.

EARLY AIRCRAFT CARRIERS

All of the various kinds of ships can and often do work together. That makes the U.S. Navy a powerful fighting force. At the close of World War II, a former secretary of the Navy says, that force "was in total control of the seas." The Navy was also "held in awe by the world." Many experts agree that this is still the case.

The birth of the aircraft carrier took place in November 1910. The Navy built a wooden platform on the bow of a warship near the Virginia coast. American pilot Eugene Ely flew a small plane off the platform. Ely almost plunged into the water. But he managed to pull the plane up just in time. In January 1911 he landed the plane on a similar platform. The test flights showed that aircraft carriers were possible.

CHAPTER **SIX:**

NAVY SPECIAL OPERATIONS

The U.S. Navy has two units of special fighters, in addition to its standard sailors. The men are part of the Naval Special Warfare Command. Its home base is near San Diego, California. Probably the best known of the units is the Navy SEALs. The other is the Special Warfare Combatant-craft Crewmen, known by its initials SWCC (pronounced "swick"). They routinely carry out special operations. So they are often called special ops for short.

These elite fighters perform missions that are too hard for ordinary sailors.

The missions require incredibly difficult training and dedication. Their official website sums up their noble creed. "In times of war or uncertainty," it says, "there is a special breed of warrior." He is "ready to answer our nation's call." Further, "I will never quit." Our nation "expects me to be physically harder and mentally stronger than my enemies." So "if knocked down, I will get back up, every time. I will draw on every remaining ounce of strength" to "accomplish our mission."

SEAL training at Camp Pendleton, California

THE NAVY SEALS

SEALs use camouflage to blend in with their surroundings.

SEAL stands for "Sea, Air, Land." It means that the men are trained to fight in all three of these places. The SEALS carry out risky, difficult missions.

They approach enemy positions under water, for example. Oftentimes they parachute to a target. After reaching it they may spy on it or destroy it. The SEALs also rescue American hostages and seek out and kill enemy leaders.

Members of SEAL teams, which are only open to men, must be in top-notch shape both physically and mentally. They endure extremely hard training. The first part lasts seven weeks. Each week the recruits perform punishing exercises. They begin by doing at least 42 pushups in less than 2 minutes. Immediately after that they do 50 sit-ups in less than 2 minutes. Six pull-ups come next, followed by a 1 ½-mile (2.4-km) run in less than 11 ½ minutes. In the fourth week of training, recruits perform even harder tests. Because of the tough tests and the fact that the recruits are not allowed to sleep much during that period, it is called hell week.

HELL WEEK

Combat crewmen showed off SEAL capabilities during a demonstration.

So-called hell week lasts a bit more than five days. Enormously hard, it tests the SEAL trainees' physical and mental reserves to the utmost. They are constantly on the move, performing difficult tasks. The trainees get plenty of food but nearly no sleep. And they are almost constantly wet and cold. Many trainees quit before the end of the grueling week.

In the second phase of training, the SEALs become champion swimmers and scuba divers. The third phase lasts seven weeks. In it the recruits learn how to use many lethal weapons, including sniper rifles. They also become explosives experts. In addition, Navy SEALs learn how to parachute from airplanes and perform first aid. They also must know how to fight and survive in all kinds of terrain. Part of that survival consists of the art of camouflage—staying hidden in any setting.

The Navy's other special ops group, SWCC, is sometimes called the Special Boat Units (SBU). But the members call themselves simply the "Boat Guys." They master the use of small watercraft for special missions. Often they ferry one or more units of SEALs into enemy territory. The Boat Guys also perform difficult sea rescues. Sometimes they must fight the enemy up close, like the SEALs do. So members of SWCC go through much of the same training as the SEALs.

Members of both Navy special ops units are proud of their history. The sacrifices of those who came before inspire them. So does meeting their country's needs, no matter how difficult. The final section of their creed states:

"Brave men have fought and died building the proud tradition and feared reputation that I am bound to uphold. In the worst of conditions, the legacy of my teammates steadies my resolve and silently guides my every deed. I will not fail."

BIRTH OF NAVY SPECIAL OPS ● ● ● ● ● ● ● ● ● ● ●

The Navy's special ops groups were inspired by units that fought in World War II. During that conflict naval leaders had a problem. They needed a few fighters to secretly scout enemy ports and ships. The men had to get very close and remain hidden. If they could blow up some of the enemy facilities, all the better. But no U.S. sailors or soldiers had the special training required for such missions. So the Navy and Army created a group of highly trained commandos. They called them the Scouts and Raiders.

In 1961 President John F. Kennedy saw a similar need. He approved the formation of new commando units. The first Navy SEAL units appeared in 1962. The first Special Boat Units evolved in the mid-1960s during the Vietnam War.

CHAPTER SEVEN:

THE U.S. NAVY IN ACTION

Sailors of the U.S. Navy have served in every one of America's wars. Some lost their lives. But the majority returned home to a thankful country.

The general public will never know the names of most of these sailors. A handful did become famous war heroes, however. One of the best known was John Paul Jones. He commanded the flagship of the Navy's first fleet during the American Revolution. That vessel engaged a British warship in battle. The enemy captain asked his American counterpart if he was ready to surrender.

Jones loudly replied, "I have not yet begun to fight!" In the end it was the British captain who gave up.

Captain John Paul Jones

Dorie Miller receiving the Navy Cross

ambushed by the Japanese at Pearl Harbor in 1941. During the attack he rushed up on deck. He had never been trained in the use of the big anti-aircraft deck guns, but he grabbed one anyway. Miller fired at the enemy planes continuously until he ran out of bullets. The Navy later awarded him a medal for his courage.

Another U.S. naval hero made his mark in the War of 1812. He was Captain James Lawrence. After he was seriously wounded, he told his officers, "Don't give up the ship!" His words became a rallying cry for other American sailors in the war.

Some of the greatest Navy heroes served in World War II. One was an African-American cook named Dorie Miller. He was aboard one of the ships

THE PT-109

One of finest American naval heroes later became president. During World War II John F. Kennedy commanded a small torpedo boat, the PT-109. One night a Japanese destroyer crashed into it. The shaken crew ended up in the water. Despite his own injuries, Kennedy managed to save most of his men. Years later, in 1961, he became the 35th U.S. president.

Edward "Butch" O'Hare was another World War II hero. A Navy pilot, his date with destiny came in February 1942. A large group of Japanese bombers neared the U.S carrier *Lexington*. O'Hare single-handedly attacked the enemy planes. He blew five of them out of the sky before more U.S. planes arrived to help. O'Hare's brave acts saved the carrier. A grateful nation renamed Chicago's airport O'Hare Airport in his honor.

NIMITZ'S VICTORIES

One of the most accomplished Navy officers in World War II was Chester W. Nimitz (left). He graduated from the U.S. Naval Academy in 1905 and worked his way up through the Navy's ranks. After the bombing of Pearl Harbor, the Navy made Nimitz commander of the Pacific fleet. He defeated the Japanese in the Battle of the Coral Sea in 1942. Other wins for Nimitz followed. Greatest of all was in the Battle of Leyte Gulf in October 1944. Some experts have called it the biggest naval battle in history. The enemy lost 27 major vessels, including four aircraft carriers. The victory paved the way for an attack on Japan's home islands.

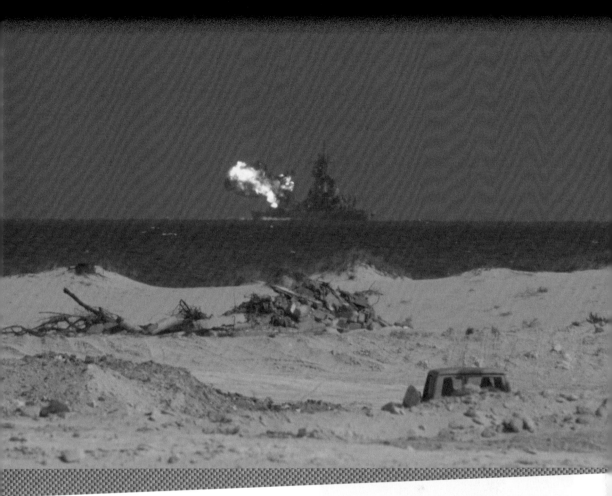

The USS *Missouri* destroyed Iraqi tanks and personnel carriers during the Persian Gulf War.

World War II had the largest number of big naval battles in history. But the Navy also saw action in later conflicts, including the 1991 Persian Gulf War. Iraq's leader, Saddam Hussein, seized the tiny nearby nation of Kuwait. Soon the United States and its allies decided to free Kuwait.

Six U.S. Navy battle groups arrived off Iraq's coast. Some of the ships fired cruise missiles at Iraqi military targets. Others kept the U.S Army supplied during its land operations. Still other ships became floating hospitals for wounded soldiers. Meanwhile, Navy planes attacked enemy tanks and buildings.

More recently Navy special ops units made history. On September 11, 2001, the terrorist group al-Qaeda struck U.S. soil. At the order of their leader, Osama bin Laden, al-Qaeda members hijacked airliners. Two struck the World Trade Center towers in New York City. Another slammed into the Pentagon in Washington, D.C.

American forces searched for bin Laden for years. But he remained safely hidden. Early in 2011 his hunters finally found him. Bin Laden was living in a small town in Pakistan. President Barack Obama ordered a unit of Navy SEALs to capture or kill bin Laden. The SEALs secretly trained for the mission for at least several weeks.

Then, on May 2, 2011, the SEALs boarded helicopters. The craft approached bin Laden's hideout in the dark of night. The commandos first fought with and killed two men on the ground floor. They may have been guarding the al-Qaeda leader. Then the SEALs found bin Laden on an upper floor. They shot him in the head, killing him instantly. Later American

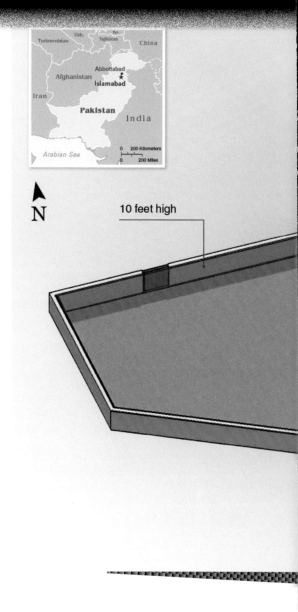

10 feet high

forces buried him at sea. To respect bin Laden's religion, they followed strict Islamic tradition in handling his body.

News of bin Laden's death quickly spread across the world. The American

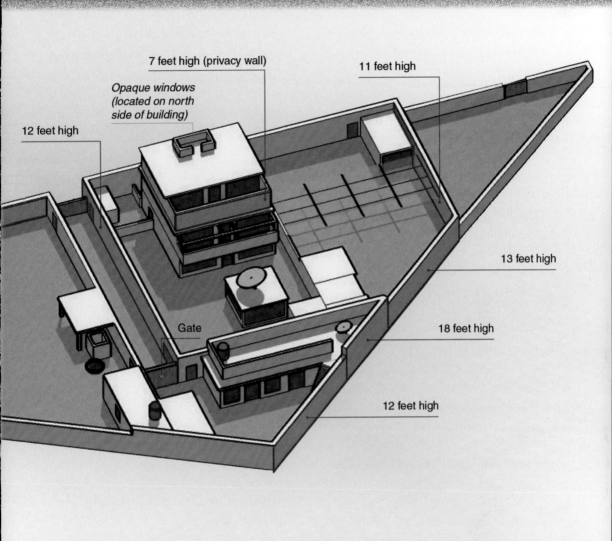

7 feet high (privacy wall)

*Opaque windows
(located on north
side of building)*

11 feet high

12 feet high

13 feet high

Gate

18 feet high

12 feet high

people heaved a collective sigh of relief.
President Obama said that justice had
been done at last. He called it "the most
significant achievement to date in our
nation's effort to defeat al-Qaeda."

**A model of the hideout
where SEALs found Osama
bin Laden in Abbottabad**

GLOSSARY

aircraft carrier—a large Navy ship with a flight deck on which airplanes take off and land

biological—when used in a naval situation, having to do with germs, sickness caused by germs, or germ weapons

capital ship—a large-scale Navy warship, most often an aircraft carrier

chain of command—the ladder of military ranks, including civilian leaders

civilian—a person who is not in the armed forces

commando—an elite, specially trained sailor or soldier who is assigned to difficult, dangerous missions

communal—shared by everyone in a given group

cruise missile—a small but lethal missile that flies close to ground level and can be programmed to strike a small, faraway target

cruiser—a large Navy ship armed with cruise missiles, big guns, and other powerful weapons

destroyer—a mid-sized Navy ship that travels fast and is armed with missiles and attack helicopters

ensign—the lowest ranking of the officers in the Navy

fleet—all of the Navy ships in a given region of the world

flotilla—a naval group consisting of a few noncapital ships

frigate—a small Navy ship that moves fast and is armed with torpedoes and attack helicopters

radioactive—having to do with materials that give off potentially harmful invisible rays or particles

seaman—an ordinary sailor; the lowest ranked enlisted sailor in the Navy

squadron—a naval group consisting of a few capital ships

task force—a group of ships of mixed types, most often including one aircraft carrier; also called a battle group

torpedo boat—a small naval vessel equipped with a few small torpedoes

SOURCE NOTES

Chapter 1: A Fearsome Force

Page 4, col. 2, line 2: John Costello. *The Pacific War*. New York: Harper and Row, 2009, p. 135.

Page 6, line 15: "Navy Organization." 23 Oct. 2012. www.navy.mil/navydata/organization/org-top.asp

Chapter 2: Navy Organization and Jobs

Page 12, col. 2, line 14: "Careers and Jobs." 23 Oct. 2012. www.navy.com/careers/

Chapter 3: Enlisting in the Navy

Page 16, line 4: Irving Berlin. "We Saw the Sea." 23 Oct. 2012. http://lyricsplayground.com/alpha/songs/w/wesawthesea.shtml

Chapter 4: Training to Become a Sailor

Page 24, line 13: "Navy Department Library: Sailor's Creed." 23 Oct, 2012. www.history.navy.mil/library/online/creed.htm

Page 26, line 5: Scott A. Ostrow. *A Guide to Joining the Military*. Lawrenceville, N.J.: Peterson, 2004, p. 157.

Chapter 5: Navy Gear, Ships, and Weapons

Page 33, line 6: John Lehman. *On Seas of Glory: Heroic Men, Great Ships, and Epic Battles of the American Navy*. New York: Free Press, 2001, p. 292.

Chapter 6: Navy Special Operations

Page 34, col. 2, line 3: "Forged by Adversity." 23 Oct. 2012. www.sealswcc.com/navy-seals-ethos.aspx#.T1epSvVvr8Y

Page 37, col. 2, line 9: Ibid.

Chapter 7: The U.S. Navy in Action

Page 38, col. 2, line 1: "Famous Navy Quotes: Who Said Them and When." 23 Oct. 2012. www.history.navy.mil/trivia/trivia02.htm

Page 39, line 5: Ibid.

Page 43, line 3: "How U.S. Forces Killed Osama bin Laden." CNN. 2 May 2011. 23 Oct. 2012. http://articles.cnn.com/2011-05-02/world/bin.laden.raid_1_bin-compound-terrorist-attacks?_s=PM:WORLD

READ MORE

Dolan, Edward F. *Careers in the U.S. Navy.*
New York: Marshall Cavendish Benchmark, 2010.

Montana, Jack. *Navy SEALs.* Broomall, Pa.:
Mason Crest Publishers, 2011.

Rudolph, Jessica. *Today's Navy Heroes.*
New York: Bearport, Pub., 2012.

White, Steve. *Naval Warship: FSF-1 Sea Fighter.*
New York: Children's Press, 2007.

INTERNET SITES

Use FactHound to find Internet sites related to this book. All of the sites on FactHound have been researched by our staff.

Here's all you do:

Visit *www.facthound.com*

Type in this code: 9780756546175

America's Navy
www.navy.com/joining.html
A site designed to start the Navy enlistment process

U.S. Navy.com
www.usnavy.com/
A site designed to provide general information about the Navy and help potential enlistees make up their minds

Military Spot.com
www.militaryspot.com/enlist/join-the-navy/
A site that explains how to join the Navy and offers advice about how to speak to a recruiter and how to submit an application

TITLES IN THIS SERIES:

TODAY'S U.S. **AIR FORCE**

TODAY'S U.S. **ARMY**

TODAY'S U.S. **MARINES**

TODAY'S U.S. **NATIONAL GUARD**

TODAY'S U.S. **NAVY**

INDEX

ABOUT THE AUTHOR

Award-winning historian and writer Don Nardo has published many books for young people. A number of them cover various aspects of military history, including overviews of many of America's wars and studies of warfare and military weapons in ancient, medieval, and modern times. Nardo lives with his wife, Christine, in Massachusetts.